GALL

MATT HOWARD

THE RIALTO

ACKNOWLEDGEMENTS

Acknowledgements are due to the editors of the following publications, in which a number of these poems, some in earlier versions, previously appeared: *Agenda*, *The Clearing*, *The Compass Magazine*, *The Dark Horse*, *The Fenland Reed*, *Lighthouse*, *The Literateur*, *Magma*, *The Morning Star*, *New Statesman*, *New Walk Magazine*, *The North*, *Plumwood Mountain*, *Poetry Ireland Review*, *The Poetry Review*, *Poetry Salzburg Review*, *The Rialto* and *Stand*. Some poems are taken from my Eyewear pamphlet, *The Organ Box*.

Note:
The last lines of 'Dispersal' reference the song *A Nightingale Sang in Berkeley Square by* Eric Maschwitz / Manning Sherwin © Sony/ATV Music Publishing LLC, Shapiro Bernstein & Co. Inc.

I owe a debt of gratitude to many who have helped this collection come together: Edward Doegar, Martin Figura, Joanna Guthrie, Andrea Holland, Colin Hughes, Helen Ivory, Emily Mayhew, Andrew McDonnell, Esther Morgan, Jonathan Morley, Les Robinson, Jos Smith, Jean Sprackland, Nick Stone, Todd Swift, Michael Symmons Roberts and Tom Warner.

A further thank you to The Poetry Trust and the 2014 Aldeburgh 8, and to the Cambridge Conservation Initiative for hosting me as their first Poet in Residence.

My deepest thanks go to three friends central to all this: John Fanshawe, Mark Cocker and Michael Mackmin. Thanks to John for his unstinting support, and to Mark, not just for Blackwater Carr but for all the rough eloquence of our conversations. And of course to Michael, for his especially patient friendship, encouragement and editing, all making this book possible.

First Published in 2018
The Rialto c/o 74 Britannia Road, Norwich, NR1 4HS

ISBN 978-1-909632-08-0

The publisher also acknowledges financial assistance from Grants for the Arts.

The Rialto is a Registered Charity No. 297553
Typeset in Berling Roman 10pt on 12.5pt leading
Art Direction and Design by Starfish Norwich
Cover image derived from a photo by Mark Cocker
Printed in England by Page Bros, Norwich, Norfolk
Author photo: Nick Stone

LOTTERY FUNDED

My love and gratitude to Amanda for everything.

CONTENTS

A JAR OF MOLES

I have trawled the whole city for your gift,
trusted the knowledge of black cabs to bring you this -
it is quite full, so be careful of its weight.

The man couldn't say how many it contains,
simply that it's full because it has to be,
just as a true heart only ever brims with love.

Each side is crammed with quiet wild faces,
pink snouts clear from their maze of dark chambers;
see, this one here still bares its teeth.

The labouring velvet behind blown glass through decades
and where one man made that emptiness
another has worked hard to fill it.

So take these moles darling, with my love,
hold them safe, and away from the sun,
cherish each heavy earth-swimming hand.

MAKING EVELYN'S TABLES

Omnia explorate; meliora retinete

It begins with a crime, a man dead,
outside of God. Then the felling of an evergreen,
a pine, from this they will make planks,
with tongue and groove to bind them, glued
with animal collagen from skin, tendon, hooves.
Last, a varnish: honey, cedar or poppy oil.

The man will be pinned in preparation,
his veins, nerves, arteries, set in a triptych.
He will display, like a winter birch, each branch
bare of fruit, the crown wracked.
In the absence of viscera he will abstract
to the spaces between bone and flesh.

Then we will truly behold a man
for ourselves; trace the inner workings,
the circuit that oxygenates blood;
the sympathetic system of fight or flight,
endings that cause sweats, the heart to race,
stripped into lines of his feeling.

GALL INK

The first arse-end backing up to an oak bud
to lay its egg with a squeeze, was a drop in a well,
an epochal and aeonic punt, and off it went
bothering out amongst all those branchings.

And you have to think how the hell exactly
it crossed the wasp's mind, stirred its wing-veins
and spiracles, which in themselves are no small things –
then that, *you know, this might just work*

and suddenly there's this gall. But what to do with it
when the wasp's done? Like anything, I guess
they were then *there*, so you burn and eat some, glean
it's good for your own diarrhoea, mouth ulcers,

aches and bleeds. Noting mixable astringent qualities
someone arrives at iron, water, gum arabic
then *I must get this down* so starts scratching it all out
on the inside of a goat's or calf's skin,

an inky flow of wasp-flared oak tissues, reams
of contracts, hymns, deeds, inventories
etc., etc., – all the what was or is to be done
and when, exactly, payment falls due.

THE GREEN CHILDREN
(Historia Rerum Anglicarum, William of Newburgh, 1150)

In East Anglia there is a village
at some distance from the noble monastery
of our Blessed King and Martyr
and near this place are ancient earthworks,
the wolf pits, where one miraculous day
two children were found, a boy and a girl.

Barefoot, clothed in the strangest colours
and unknown hides, with a ferny
character to their skin, they were seized
by the reapers and conducted to the village.
They crossed the fields in bewilderment
and went many days without food.

But whilst nearly exhausted with hunger
and yet unable to relish any kindness,
when beans were given to them from the field,
feeling merely the hollowness of their stalks
they howled with the bitterness of wolves
and ate only when given the pulses.

They fought but learned the fortitude of bread
then through natural effects of our food,
changed colour by degrees and acquired our language.
It seemed fitting they received the sacrament
of baptism. The boy survived but a little time. The girl lived,
though through her respectable years was asked always

of where she came. She is said to have replied:
There was comfort, of a dream I cannot remember
then this sound, as we are now accustomed to hear
of the chiming of the bells at St Edmunds
and we were then entranced amongst you
in the fields in a moment where you were reaping.

What I most want to say is, in our country
there were different divisions, infinite
curiosity. We did not know in any words
I can recount now. Not sun, or twilight,
a luminous country, a vast endless river
and somehow not at all far from here.

REDWOOD

If I buy the idea of my very birth-cry as a release of carbon,
a vagrancy of atoms that spread evenly in the atmosphere, taking
      eighteen months
with any immeasurable amount of ins and outs, then let's consider a sequoia.

And let us say that some part of that squawk was locked in, on a hillside
that today is facing the calm Pacific. The Golden Gate is open, traffic flowing
and a family is wandering in the shade, on the boardwalk trail below

amongst the root system. May all their love go unspoken. Despite other
      consumables,
box sets, fags, chemical foods, all the shit tricks and distractions,
      multitudinous dispersals
from every argument before or since, let's stay with that first cry. Say it went
      through an air-con vent

rushing around the baggage claim at Marco Polo, or, comingling again,
      both plant and animal,
via some metabolic functions – a migratory duck's arse, a banana slug
      at work on its stool.
But then if we consider our fate on this earth is truly written in the stars
      beyond this biosphere,

imagine the scream feeding back in the questionable air miles of your
      morning fruit;
perhaps a prior harvest, when pap was sucked through the uncoiled
      proboscis of a Monarch
or other butterfly, somewhere in the Coffee Belt; or in the bean now
      scorching down your oesophagus -

those first few carbon atoms that have gone, entirely unsequestered,
      overheating machines
in the paper mills, creased then pulped from folds of cards for one
      occasion or another.
Let me pay it further forward: Happy all our Birthdays; for now, at least
      some part of my legacy is tree.

GORILLA GORILLA GORILLA
For Guy

For his moods, the schemes and theories behind each curious held gaze,
the gasps and beating of his chest; for his hands, their absolute power
and grace; every capture and release of sparrow or finch – unharmed,
     their flight intensified.

For his obesity, each of his thirty-four stones, and his teeth,
spoiled with melon, pineapple and dates, even punnets of strawberries,
     sent out of season.
For his thirty one years and the necessary dentistry that killed him.

For his dead weight in the deep freeze, his pelt in the tanning drum,
the shrinkage of his skin and the beatitudes in his DNA;
     the silver of his back
that would not stretch for the stitching. Guy on his haunches
     as full-mounted specimen.

For all the incinerated viscera, the vanished waters of his eyes,
     their empty sockets;
for the painted glass beads and the person who came
     by Circle Line to deliver them
and everyone they reflect; the irises too brown, the too-perfect
     ring of each limbus.

TO AN ANATOMICAL VENUS

Lady, you have no chest,
no stomach; the curtain of muscle
drawn, you are a reliquary, a trinket box,
faithful cavity of delicacies.

I pick out liver, kidney, spleen –
petals of your carnation, the heart
bright as a leaf from any book of hours.
Your maker has served you well.

I cannot meet your gaze or parted lips.
The comb of vessels on these neat lungs
suggests held breath, a promise -

a host of wax, braided with a wick
of real hair. I will not lift your womb;
the foetus, its honeyed silence.

CLOUTIES AT MADRON

August sweating the fields and water.
The reek of last night's rain, something larval
through the baptistery; a roofless pest house
where gnats bite, red-eyed flies rub legs
and beetles busy in the joints of the walls.

While you sat and closed your eyes
I heard the thin cry of a luckless shrew,
and wind stirred that thorn bower -
its chasuble of rags scrabbling, all knotted higher,
each at the cost of someone else's child.

DACHA
Vršac Hill

A wedding gift or inheritance
with a curious attitude to the finish,
only part-rendered, half-shuttered, all desire
for maintenance spun thin as this baler twine
staying the unlocked but glossed front gate.

Imagine the aspect in summer: laughter
in the shade of the veranda; cicadas;
grapes swelling on the thickening vines.

I am fifteen hundred miles away,
there is three-day-old snow, here, at the end
of the sharpest incline and this is the view:

the morning is still breaking down the dog-leg
of the hillside, mist burning off deepening altitudes -
sky, scrub, vineyards marrying into this January day
with something, old, new, borrowed and blue
as any of the distances in me.

THE HOUSE OF OWLS

The Founding of the House of Owls

Before the many mothers, before the house,
her: she came with a heavy scent of hawthorn,
and all men were taken by her owl-white skin,

by her silent graces. She took just one
to the far meadow. He went meek as a harvest mouse.
Her garland of bluebell and yellow archangel slipped,

she tied his wrists with bindweed,
snicked stems of Jacob's-ladder for their pillow.
On that unbroken earth she whispered:

Here we will have our many sons and daughters,
this is land to be taken, good ground for us to claim.
With each dead-nettle kiss she laid on his neck

a clutch of welts raised, never faded.
And in their parish, this we know:
that ruin of a house still stands.

The True Heir of the House of Owls

Born wrong, with an insatiable gape
and one odd tooth in a mask of a face.
It didn't so much cry as screech,

craved only for meat, begged
then swallowed whole. When it did settle,
it was into squeaks, snorts, hisses.

This first born came between them,
turned their bed into a midden,
a heap of fur, tails and tiny skulls.

He hadn't been near her in weeks,
when she caught him, three fields over,
whistling up at the lark, it was too far.

She waited with the child in its high chair
for when he came in that night, reeking of meadows -
met him with her black-marble stare:

Here my love, is how a head can turn.
And with one hand on its shoulder,
one on the crown, she took that shrieking head,

twisted it past all turning.

A Vision of Order at the House of Owls

It was scryed again in the belly of a strung-up pig.
They would have acres, far as the eye could see,
grazed and under plough; an estate for generations.

They worked hard for this gift.
Stone by insufferable stone, by the roots
of each felled tree; broke their backs every day.

He beasted a hound for coursing;
perfected the deadfall, birdlime and pole traps,
acquired breech-loading rifles.

He hanged one of each dead singer
from that immovable oak, where he carved her name
with those of all their children, born and yet to come.

The Fall of the House of Owls, 1914

The man that came to cap the chimney stack
back then would have crossed a muddle of fields,
where his good word had beaten the bounds before him.
'Just a simple fix', he told her, 'a rough tile to point in'.
He marked year and initials by the trace of his fingertip.
By the smallest touches a house can fall.

A white feather chased two sons away,
then the front door lintel pocked with holes
where they say the mother, mad with hope,
nailed countless barn owl carcasses. Fields widened
and trunk roads drew close to the old routeways
where so many, blown sidewards, come to grief.

A century later contractors have come
and emptied the stack. A full three barrows -
fallout of desiccated abundance; pellets crammed
with all that went with the meadows and hedgerows:
relics of frog, yellowhammer, dormouse,
Natterer's bat, water shrew, weasel.

The Deliverer of the House of Owls

She has lived too long this way,
so old, deep into the monoculture of age.
On the brink like a slack-necked hatchling,

her bruised scalp flecked with white down
and the dangled quiver of those wasted arms -
one cold, wet wind could dash her away now.

On occasional days they bring her back,
though she can no longer make the stairs,
just sits in her chair by the picture window.

In between sleeps her sunken face looks out,
twisted to the mute brown-green blur of fields.
And no word from her for nearly five years.

Yet that last night she woke the house with a shriek,
swore she saw, with her bad eye, a luminous owl
lit with honey fungus, flying the bounds of their acreage.

STASH

We had the run of the wood,
could whittle and burn anything.
Each of us with a hand-picked knife
that had to have loopholes for the belt
and a lace to tie it to your thigh.
For those two or three years we went unseen.

Then there was that smell of wet rot,
a heap of beer cans, ring-pulls,
Rizlas and dog-ends; gorse still yellow
back up the lane. A tang
of hawthorn flowering. The cut
of the women's hair caught us

in a silence, held too open,
too close while we huddled.
One of us knew more, called it *Grot*,
and something else that sounded cruel.
We were already late. There'd be trouble
for the pockets full of acorns,

all the muck, twigs and stones
carried back in our turn-ups;
for the stink of green wood-smoke –
bloody filthy. I stripped on the doorstep,
screened by a hornbeam hedge
close to the right side of the house.

I looked out of my window past dark
that night. I couldn't stop thinking
of those reddish, budding leaves,
all their folds, soft and whiskery
and shiny; how would they look tomorrow;
how I wanted to, but dared not touch.

MAGGOT-MOUTH

He'd warm maggots, roll them
on the tongue behind his teeth,
then sling fistfuls to bait a swim.

With an old-bastard laugh in all weathers,
bait box breath and lung rattle,
and his gog on the bankside sedge

yellow as the innards of split casters.
He'd slide them with the meat of his thumb
past the barb on too-big hooks.

I would have been eleven or twelve
that August, when fear itself was maggots
slipped into your coat hood or pockets,

the stink and taste of them
in your lunch box; those new-hatched,
writhing in the side of a dead tench.

And then there was the story of that girl,
washed to him at the crook of the river
one dawn, that he staked her to the bank

with an old iron rod-rest, then carried on.
Unreasonably young someone said,
and something about her *still open eyes*.

All I knew in that quease of a summer
was how quickly a maggot turns to caster,
how casters burst into flies.

FEMUR
La Boisselle, 1/6/08

Tommy bone or Bosche bone?
Held against my own, a short man's thigh bone
sheared below the hip; spiked scrap of bone,
blown bone; exhumed bone
lost from the rest, (killed twice); dumped bone.

Officer's bone or Private's bone?
Killer's bone? Husband's or father's bone?
Salt of the earth or bastard's bone?
A dead mother's loved bone.
A picked-up-stick of bone

regimental never demobbed; bone
memory, bone immemorial, bone
utterly without irony, bone
without epiphany - bone,
only a short man's thigh bone.

SONG THRUSH
Les coquelicots B&B, Pozieres

He can barely fly. His khaki fatigues
soaked through, strung neck swathed
under beads; the one thrush seen all day.

Now, after incendiary sun, leaden rain,
there's only him singing to the premature dusk
over these fields and a handful of shuttered houses.

Here weather mobilises fast. Pressure
fronts collide over the open ground.
On the *circuit de souvenir* land is so fertile -

the earth must till itself.
Each season looses more swallowed
ordnance, still fused, for clearing.

After four-egg omelettes we play pool,
watch the teatime news in French.
He's out there, still on the wire in the dark,

head gone, cold rain rising in hollow bones
singing; not for romance or what's behind
or ahead; a pure lyric for his moment only,

just a chance a chance a chance.

A WONDERFUL BOY
After Miguel Hernández

Who lit his own birth with the ferocity of orange blossom
Who cried with grief's voice, of the quick ways of love and the knife
Who grew in the dilated wound of his people.

Who played at ease in the goat herd
Who listened at the she-goat's belly
Who heard the beginnings of milk coming to her udders.

Who climbed each tree in the orange grove, whistling
Who showed the émigré, Neruda, just how a nightingale sings
Who gave humanity all that the song foretells.

Who knew rhetoric is blown glass
Who crafted that element in the heart's deeds
Who blew a sad fishbowl of dying nightingales.

Who had too much heart
Who slept like any man or goat, worth the whole of the earth
Who dreamed of history, the blood moon, even as it set in his chest.

Who resides in that street with all our sons
Who grow in the unruly water of the cemetery
Who they had to bury with eyes beautifully open.

TODAY IN THE STARVING CITY OF OUR LIBERATION

No fish have been spared in the aquarium.
Rumours persist about the disappearance of cats.
That priest returned with his pocketful of denunciations,
requested a pistol and a permit to carry it.

Three sisters with their heads shaved came from the hills,
reported something untranslatable regarding *time with the priest*
and were positively tremulous with some passion or injustice;
they left cider, or bad wine, and one blood-spotted egg.

The search of the catacombs continued
amidst accounts of knocking and scratching.
An obstinate monk was removed by force
and is now held in our cells on a charge of hoarding rats.

While the Mayor insisted with further papers of pure invention,
he left nothing but the smell of vegetables or dry rot
and claimed I wore the face of a hypocrite.
(I now fear all the more for the thinning flanks of his horse).

Just past lunch there was a bomb blast at the post office,
a time delayed fuse. One hundred dead. A tragedy –
so much plaster dust spoiled the raw flesh
of each halved tomato sun-drying in our courtyard.

'IF YOUR PICTURES AREN'T GOOD ENOUGH, YOU'RE NOT CLOSE ENOUGH'
Robert Capa

I've been thinking about Capa's Loyalist soldier
falling into his own shadow, whether or not to believe
his heart burst into that white shirt the moment after
the shutter clicked; such *serious business* to follow.

Faces crowded at the Morgue gates in Valencia
imploring the lens of a Leica for news; the pure ferocity
in a seven year-old's look, consoling her grandmother;
La Pasionaria and the farewell for the International Brigades.

Yet I've been thinking mostly of Taro, before Spain, captured by Capa:
beautiful exile, pulling faces; a wink, goofy, shy, then unaware
at the May Day parade, smiling, buying Lily of the Valley,

the closest he ever got, frame after frame of her sleeping;
all the packed suitcases of Europe for a pillow –
whether anything can ever be so grievous as love.

FROM NATURAL HISTORY
After Pliny the Elder

Vedius Pollio, equestrian of Rome
and councillor for the late Emperor Augustus,
kept a tankful of lampreys from northern Gaul.
They each had seven shining spots on their right jaw,
aligned like the Plough in the Great Bear,
though that asterism fades when they die.

He had condemned slaves thrown to the lampreys,
not because land-beasts were incapable,
but his pitch-sealed tank was so suspended
to afford fullest orbit of the bodies being harrowed;
the flurry, arterial and venous, all dark matter –
how gravity is unfixed by rings of teeth.

THE BALLAD OF THE BOOK OF ADDERS

The face on my frontispiece
is my dead twin brother's,
killed only one month old
by a cold fanged adder.

Mother was picking furze flowers
that first spring of our lives,
the viper had both, him then her,
only I survive.

She lived ten and five further years,
poor long-rotted mother,
bit blind, undone by grievous tears,
for my stone-dead other.

And she never lost her baby weight,
her skin stayed bloated, livid,
and the last thing she saw was a slither away,
a bitch of a snake that was gravid.

Father wanted more sons,
Mother gave no more,
he near-drowned himself in cider
then ran off with the hagfish next door.

So this book is more than my life
it began before I could crawl,
the boards are my Father's boot soles
wrapped in my brother's shawl

and the spine is from that festered heath,
roots and stems of gorse
bound by my mother's hair,
all set without remorse.

I've burned many hundred heaths
across the breadth of England,
and I'd scorch however many hundred more,
acres of orchid, whin, bracken.

Each page of this book is adder skin
for I've had many of her kind,
and though I've never caught her yet,
I'm just the odd sloughed skin behind.

While I've never known a woman's touch
in my seventy years of days,
I know the track of that zig-zag back,
the slink of all her ways.

Here are pages of her eyeless eyes,
her empty venomous cowls,
blind to the shrugged off lives she leaves
and all the sorrows she's uncoiled.

So I'll hound her to the far coast wall,
breach dunes to the boiling sea,
and I'll whisper to her inner ears:
come roll fathoms down with me,

for we are all done now,
for we are all done now.

CONCERNING THE MOTION OF THE HEART AND BLOOD IN LIVING CREATURES

Whilst accepting the findings of vivisection,
all the openings of dogs, eels, toads and ravens,
mysteries of the heart and blood of man remained.

Now hastened to Court was a young noble who had fallen,
fracturing ribs on the left side of his breast;
Providence brought abscess, putrefaction left such a void

that before them was the living heart,
its ventricles in pulsation
only part eclipsed in the zodiac of a chest.

Via simple observance, the beating seat of a soul,
all feeling of a loyal subject in microcosm,
and the full heat from this little sun sworn to the King's.

His Majesty's Inspector of Anatomy,
master of the dark side of the healer's art,
directed the King's own hand into the wound.

Three fingers and the Royal right thumb then divined,
found only muscle, working, devoid of all sense or deference;
the noble remained unmoved as if untouched.

Whilst physicians rhapsodised at this organ,
its clear function, active only when expelling blood,
the King retired to his private chamber,

proclaimed some malady from the waxing moon,
chilled as if a run of elvers were slithering to his nape
and his head pounding with a sudden baying of hounds.

SIR, WE HAVE FIVE MINUTES UNTIL WE'RE LIVE

Ok, ok, so it's time for me to talk.
Here? Is this the line where I best hit the mark?

I'll need a lectern, somewhere to hide the hands –
of course I'll relay the lesson learned, *I understand*

all the hurt caused; and a glass of still water,
something to hold, to allow some small gesture,

if you please. I'll open being contrite
but stick to the agenda, be forthright –

yes, yes, *I'm the offender*
but point to the future, remember

that above all; what else can I say?
Thanks for watching, good night, God bless. Ok!

SQUANDER BUG

This is my uncle's seventy year-old doodle,
the Squander Bug still stuck,
though yellowed and foxed, on the top of the chest.
Every box inside is crammed with eggs,

there must be one of each species to be found
a bike ride's radius around Deopham.
All have the date and place they were taken,
some with an extra note, like the moorhen's:

From the dyke, west end of the Yank airfield.
I slipped off the branch of a rotting sallow.
Drenched, tore my trousers and rawed my knee.
Mother wholly cross when I got home.

There's a Golden Syrup tin of Coke bottle tops,
Hershey's Bar wrappers, 50 calibre casings
and a 1941 DiMaggio card –
then there are lists and dates of those other raids,

the B-17s he counted back:
The Duchess of FUBAR, Why Worry,
That's All Jack, Sunrise Serenade.
The wisecrack invention of so many names

in a receipt book of his own notation,
ticks and red ink crosses, and at the back,
under browned tape, the crushed platelets
of a skylark egg, some hair-trigger bones.

DISPERSAL

A farthing placed in the finger of a flying glove,
rabbit's feet hung in turrets and cockpits,
then seven arcs of piss over the tail wheel.
An armourer hammers the bomb doors shut
with the blunt end of an axe, *Don't worry Gents,*

we'll make her good when she's brought back.
A final green flash near the last of the light.
Ground crew, the Chaplain, and WAAFs
all leave the field, distance and dark
between them, one tries but fluffs some lines:

I may be right, I may be wrong
but I'm perfectly willing to swear

and like an echo far away,
a nightingale sings in Berkeley Square.

TOTAL RECONSTRUCTION OF THE BURNED FACE

'make a face which does not excite pity or horror.
By so doing we can restore a lost soul to normal living'.
Sir Archibald McIndoe

At all costs eyes must be kept from drying,
though streaming will need treatment in time.
Lids are too fragile, stitching them uncertain -
to blink freely cannot be understated.

Only then can we refigure the architecture
of a face, its harmony and balance,
so that the airman may blush into his skin
and smile with it, rather than beneath it.

Over decades each face will pass
under another's care; further exposure to light
brings contracture, new scars, need for running repairs

and of course we shall look, they are faces
disfigured in fire, but we must not stare:
we are trustees of each other.

WASP NEST IN A BOWLER HAT
Domine Dirige Nos

My Queen, Governors and fellow drones,
on this most arid of mornings
our new city hums in hexagonal cells. This very day,
the manufacture of paper increases exponentially.
Our vaults, and each of us, are filled with common purpose.
All futures are of course larval and we know
incidence of sting can go up or down,
yet we still promise always to pay the bearer in full.

Let this be the year of wasps, high summer
sustainable with the endless ooze of sugars;
the entitlement of wasps. Buzz with risk.

Go now, take your commission: al fresco breakfasts
of pastries and jam, then golden picnic afternoons.
Levy ice cream from the lip of every man, woman and child.

A WOMAN BREASTFEEDING IN THE NATIONAL GALLERY

is crying and no one is ashamed to look as her face slips
its makeup. Almost boneless, just days after birth, here she is
concept, object d'art. Crying a fountain by the cloakroom,
she is less *Madonna of the Pinks*, more a Pietà.

That baby, its hunger; fists full of her puffed areola,
mouth of her pistil. Lily white and straggle-veined
she strains, an Empress squeezed into her old clothes.
Everyone looks; none can say enough is enough.

A MAN HIT ON THE HEAD BY A FALLING FLOWERPOT IN ROME

On Via wherever, right by me,
in the eternal city. There was such blood,
though he was still breathing
when I reached him, wilting
in that August sun raw enough to fry an egg.

I was alone with an Italian
and couldn't understand. Confessions are hard
in a language you don't know.
Maybe he was saying how he fell
his whole life, or words for a family –

all the time me just willing he could stand,
look at me, laugh, pointing at the flowerpot.
And it would be clear
it was enough to have killed us,
fallen from god knows how far.

But there I was, holding him; past the moment
where life ends, or the soul gets up,
leaves a body and its shadow. I didn't know the man,
couldn't tell you what he said,
or even that red-petalled flower's name.

ON THE TENACITY OF LIFE

They caught it just south of the Doldrums.
Even *Half-lung*, our asthmatic Snowboy,
subject of their usual fun,
joined all hands hauling the albatross down.

In the panic, the Snowboy seized on its back.
He folded both wings, cradled the body with one arm,
and with his free hand, squeezed the flailing neck;
inched fingers to the apt part of its throat and strangled.

In the quiet moment following death
the boy found his voice. He told of the skin's value,
that from such a specimen each man could take good share –
collectors and naturalists would clamour when we made port.

As he bid, one fetched twine, bound the feet, wings and beak.
Another brought an old meat cloth to cover it
and another yet carried the corpse to the port snow trunk
to stow safely there, on the highest shelf.

For those next ten days I took pleasure to observe
how he was now joined in their laughter. *Young Ice-heart*
they called him; a small marvel, a man
given to new purpose. Our passage those days was calmer.

On the eleventh day the dead bird grunted.
At the sight of a lamp it snapped the binds
and one wing, floundered, half-frozen, then slumped
to the floor. Aghast, Half-Lung despatched it again;

he ruined the skin with stabs, the skull with his boot heel.
Two broken ribs and three teeth were then excised –
naturally the hands were moved to violence
in lieu of lost profit. He was not seen for some days.

Upon his return he displayed contrition,
offered trinkets to all: albatross
fashioned into charms, earrings, fish hooks;
crudely engraved bones of the pinions for pipe stems.

For the Captain's children he made a Sunday toy -
the bird's thorax as hull, ribs as keel,
breastbone formed the bowsprit; sealskin stretched
and fixed so that the ark would float.

The kindness given to me was a flute,
which on his effort to demonstrate usage
I took at once; his blue-lipped wheeze
and shrill notes were simply too distasteful.

THE ANATOMICAL STOREROOM INVENTORY

I kick-off with a varnished shark's heart,
lion's toes and monkey faces,

you with the whole sea-horse,
its brood pouch peeled, full of eggs.

I reel off clubfoot, tapir's anus, a shotgun blasted femur
and say how our intestines are just like sausage skin.

You suggest I'm heartless as that aortic arch
thickened with syphilitic aneurysm

and point me to *the concentric jewel* of a boar's epididymis,
the *complete votive* of a three-week old whale foetus.

I continue with a sequence of cock-sparrow testes,
though confuse the skin of bull's scrotum

with that of the finer dura mater. You tick-off foot sole,
of *Homo sapiens*, dissected, displaying roots of a callus.

REGRESSION TO THE MEAN

Equally applicable to men, brutes and plants.
Sir Francis Galton

Washing your hair, I'm always struck
how my right hand is like a calliper,
little finger and thumb, weighing your forehead.
Sick again, I have scrubbed you long enough

to exfoliate bone. Such congested eugenics
at bath time; your head lolls like a late daffodil -
your sparrow lungs are brisk with a crow's hack.
Impatient as ever, my back and calves ache.

Our ritual bickering glossolalia.
My puffed fingertips are peelable now,
a fault of the skin in water; each whorl

unfathomable as the efficacy of prayer
or how this water moves, its gravity waves
reassembling my face like a photofit.

THREE WEEKS INTO A HEAT WAVE

and the quicksilver pulse of roach or rudd
and these circles they riffle on the pool
and the jack pike passing under that spooks them
reminds me of when we were here in winter

how a hairline crack in the ice shook us
how we froze as water scuttled our boots
how the reeds we rushed to are now further out
and how a mind is a drift of roots

and nothing sits passive in its place

SUBSONG

When winter is tuned, warmed under the breath
for these days that are of more care, than carelessness;

quieter song, that comes in from the cold, like one dark-eyed
with a freshness off their hair and skin, sinuous; tried -

though less known than felt; a change in the air, breathing,
heart-rate, pupil dilation; all of this is readying

for the one true song you will remember
after the roost of your mind through November,

December; that month where you stand
scraping ice from the windscreen with an ungloved hand,

the hard miles between beginning,
before closing distances of all you'll come to sing.

TIC

Just as a tick can't be coaxed
back from a bite, out from under
the skin, where its burrowed head
is so compelled and drawn to taste,

I won't deny that when you look at me,
face to face, there's still that little stick
and twitch, that tell-tale nervousness
about your lower left eyelid.

GALLING

Take a robin's pincushion, witch's broom,
a juniper's swollen tongue of fire; even better,
go raw your knuckles knocking on an oak trunk.
Then see all this fretting, this tease, as no more

than a similar gushing forth. An ooze; an outgrowth;
a disease: clubroot, rust, powdery scab, canker,
or an egg laid in a leaf or flower bud.
So it all comes with some altering of the tissues,

the lava still unfolding within
a green, sticky chamber. And it's unflinching,
that gnawing idea of you and me,

this small, glistening thing
working a way free by sheer force
of its own mandible, maxilla and labium.

THANATOSIS

Do you remember that six foot birch stump?
Unbuttressed. An off-wind must've come,
cleaved it to that awkward height. Wanted gone
by someone; the top deep-notched by axe-blows,
daubed green with herbicide and then a ring
of seventy mil copper nails hammered in.

And do you remember that buff-tip moth,
its inch and a half of mimicry -
a snapped birch twig idling in the brashing?
All those inner mechanics, imperceptible
even to the stirrings of our little fingers,
that torpor too deep for any gentleness.

RAPTOR

He quarters there, in the blindest corner,
where the days are sinking cataracts.
That hole in the air between

where a cry is declared, faster and from higher.
And each waking since is at the end
of this long stoop; past the north saltings,

one last estuarine night, where we know
the talon of a hind toe, the working flexors
and his tiercel eyes that track us again

to this threshed-up morning; snow in the grate,
our room a mire of down and my own shrill overbite
that still seethes with love for you.

THE BLIZZARD OF BIRTH AND DEATH

I don't want to think any more
        of the one night in May
                when we were slowed to a crawl
                        as we crossed the Ebro,

or the headwind of that gale;
        mayflies on the wing,
                mating in their silken millions,
                        drawn up from the river

to the slick of streetlamps
        on smooth, dark asphalt
                and each egg laid in vain.
                        But I keep imagining

our two shadows behind
        every wave, each squall
                and pulse of wiper blades,
                        the smear of chitin

all caught in one exposure
        by some artist or masochist
                stood out there for a photograph,
                        sunk under the insects

crowding his clothes,
        nose, eyes, ears and mouth -
                I imagine him holding
                        his breath before it's taken.

ACQUIRED DEFORMITIES:
CONSTRICTION OF FEMALE THORAX
Presented by Sir Erasmus Wilson, 1884

Preserved the way you were wanted,
wasp-waisted, deformed from years of corsetry,
cartilage and ribs drawn oblique
like tight lace. The curve in the spine,
once pliable, fused here,
a lifelong pinch to angle the bust.

Diminutive even in your glass case
all I have are metaphors for you:
your wicker ribs an empty fruit basket
or a beekeeper's straw skep, colonised
then smoked out by men's words for sweetness -
caught in the vice of their love; concertina of bones.

That I could hold you now, ease this organ box,
free each reed, feel you breathe.

WHITE-CLAWED CRAYFISH

I must look up the anatomy of crayfish,
in particular, the names for the tail piece
and each lapped part up to the carapace;
the ligaments and musculature
of what I imagine is abdomen,
the softer side that contracts, curls under,
and where the female becomes berried
with eggs. How it all articulates –

the gripping force of those claws,
their range of movement. Tangled in the line
more than twenty years ago, bleached in torchlight,

she took the thick edge of a dull blade twice
and only loosed when her unbroken claw splayed.
I need to convey that expression of pain.

BLACKWATER CARR

Yield

Blackwater does not just give some simple tonnage by the acre,
all that cut wood in separate stacks under tarpaulin
left drying until it can be taken back by the boot load
to heat the whole house through however many winters.

There's the weight of everything that is uncut and still growing.
The tangled force and will in each individual cell.
Take the mycelia under seat-logs laid in a half-ring
around the trunk of the jay-sown oak; each lopped sallow

reaching with suckers; various umbellifers; geulder berries
in blistered clusters; the thickening sward of reed sweet-grass.
Then all that is larval: tree bumblebee nests, swollen-thighed beetles,
maggoty nettle-tap, or the fleshier elephant hawkmoth.

This is to say nothing of the slithery grabs of slub, cromed
from three dykes, the number of lung-heaves and gags
at the hauled-out anaerobic stink that sits somewhere between
meat and shit; bacteria reeking its first/last when brought to air.

And leftovers: raptor kills, fox kills; dragonfly cases,
that perfectly whole shed skin of a grass snake.
Or the empty two litre water bottle done before lunch
last time out, when we slumped in our chairs, good as spent

and that wren came in at eye-level; tail cocked, head lifted
with an up-thrust through each hallux, its grip perching
on the newer, nearest wood stack, piercing the trill higher.

Brashing

I'll need you for an old dog rose,
it's all scrambled up and through the sallows
at the choked dyke. It'll be hard graft,
so bring rough gloves and drink.

Scrambled up and through the sallows,
it's all thorn with no flower.
Bring your roughest gloves and drink.
Not one stem will brash –

it's all thorn with no flower,
but we'll set the fire close
and as no stem will brash
we'll burn that scrub of grief.

With the fire set close
we can make quick work of deadwood,
burn that scrub of grief,
drag it, hand over hand.

We can make quick work of deadwood.
We'll haul out our own hollow,
drag it, hand over hand
and though thorn can near wreck a man

we'll haul our own hollow.
It'll be hard graft by the choked dyke.
You know thorn can near wreck a man,
so I'll need you for that old dog rose.

Reed Sweet-Grass

A quarter acre of it, mowed
down the low meadow for the clearing.
Frost and stubble among the rides.
Dominant and too coarse to bale,
a day's work with rake and fork.

An aesthetic of summer justified
by muscle memory in February,
slung from hip, back, shoulder and wrist –
the idea of the nectar-rich; marsh orchid,
ragged robin, hemp agrimony

and what it all might mean. High talk,
but none of it bluff or bluster;
hard-pronged, our true vernacular sworn
and sweated by the good tonnage we heap,
taller than a big man. Purposeful.

The stack will grow warm as a body inside;
a hibernacula of predator and prey:
grass snake and her leathery eggs,
tunnelings for vole and shrew,
all bedfellows of the rat, three feet down.

Crome

v.

to cast a tool of ash and hooked iron

to take care in boots at the edge of standing water

to throw from the shoulder, then heave from the lumbar spine

to clear a dyke of leaf-fall and slub from the past three decades or further

to feel a suck and pop of sedge-roots tearing from bog

to spit splash-back of festered water from one's lips

to retch one's balance of vows and curses where no one else is listening

to imagine a cut of clearer water

to haul deeper with long-draw tines

to blister then callus both hands in unfavourable conditions

to consider the phased wing-strokes of dragonflies

to listen to the short, descending arc of willow warbler song whilst working

to see sunlight on the nodes of a Norfolk hawker's forewing

to act with the whole body and mean it

Snath

Heavy as the long rides to be scythed today,
a seventy year-old beechwood handle –
but still she holds perfectly; laden

as a blackcap's note, tested in late August.
By the wrong hand she'll lead or ground me,
so the right must simply follow true,

just as this afternoon planes the tops
of alders, sallows, that one oak.
She's the way to cut and meadow-make.

And sunburn, each ache, scratch and sting
is justified when felt,
live through the core and skin:

it's all a job of work; this weight of you
that dulls my blade these days,
though each night oils then swipes like a whetstone.

Sallow

For all those times when the saw blade sticks
there's a clear articulation in felling; the first bristle
and cracks as good fracture sighs away from the teeth
with no more than its own weight and you're through

into this low sun, this December shading of the shortest days,
just a handful of hours from the year's turning; all the better
to see the lengths your own body has made. Drag clear
then process. Here's wood for next winter's stack –

you must know there'll always be some burning,
though you can lop and brash the rest. And you'll feel this
into the New Year, days hence, the grip and squeeze
of all that kneading across your chest. It's a small clearing

you've made now, where months can weigh on that open ride,
its bank of bramble to flower in late May, with space and light
for whitethroat to come pitch a song flight, and the later chances -
swallowtail nectaring; the sun-dipped tips of white admiral antennae.

THE DRAWER OF KINGFISHERS

In a row of study skins, the closest thing
to the bird is this single left wing:
Shot on the jetty at Rollesby.
You can run your finger and thumb
along the curve of feather and bone –

vane and current. A water-bracer;
hilt of a king's stiletto
in a slow lowland river
that breaks with the catch; a struck match
at the corner in the blue of your eye.

LITTLE FISH

Now you've rolled up,
while you're still
gelatinous, sort of
like a salmon egg,

your nested cells
are huddling together
for this prelude, with a pulse,
forming tubes

like a fish's own inner muscle,
a double horseshoe
melding into one -
the first form of your body.

So your embryonic heart
has begun to beat and grow
and taken its place with us
amongst every vertebrate echo.

GORSE MITES

Look at this furze in December, still bursting
its own spinous boundary. Here,
where everything is dead-bracken-brown,
where low heath sweeps to reedbed, saltmarsh
then sea. And of all the ways to dream
some place in the world, on this trail
where the wind isn't up to much,
such clotted red blooms
under their self-spun billowy tent,
dew-sagged, dampening gorse-gold
with this gorgeous hoary damage.

MIDST

You have conjured me this:
January sunsets; their brevity
the richest bequest to rival
the light in a hundred Turners;
and how, on those bus rides home,
crawling past the same fields,
each day was a perceptible
turning out of night
that allowed the same trees
to be drawn ever naked,
raw, but attendant
to the movements
of jackdaws and rooks;
how, in that prevailing frost
I could see a rook's breath;
because of you, a bus ride
showed me the edge of dusk
catch passengers' faces sideways
then slip away as we turned
off, closer then, to home;
how, ten years later
your four year old grandson's
look could cut through the rings
of an oak, putting you
in a room you never walked in;
how when I shout myself awake
I hear your voice in mine.

A GLASS OF WARMED MILK BEFORE BED

Mid-February and minus five below,
so I raise this for those in labour down their earthworks,
the pink and blind, suckling in the warmth of the sett;
and for a cull on worry under strip-lighting
in the dairy sheds; for immunity of all herds;
this day done and the deeper movings of worms.

STOMATA

Thinking about oak again
and I confess I'm taken in
by the near-rhyme –

no fuss, pain,
sorrow or running sores
just, why not say it, grace and wonder.

Each one breathing: the underside
of however many thousand-odd
pinnate leaves on an oak tree;

miniscule but perceptible.
May we all live
and get away as easy.

DATUM

You left a glass of near-turned milk
by the front door as if to draw a ghost.
We had talked late and of everything.

Sleep was a cold confusion of birds,
the stuck chink of a chaffinch,
robins ticking incessant at the edge

of territory. Ice set hard as pig iron.
We walked there, found him in time
enough to barely hear movement:

grace notes of snow falling after
the fall; slips from the hedgerow –
the faint yield and hold of flakes

crumpling in the ditch bottom
where he struggled, naked as a miracle.
There was no explanation, just warm hands

on near translucent skin, his spider-work
of veins - blue crystallite blooms,
the spindly ribs borne kneading between us.

This other must have fallen clear through,
himself under some misalignment, the frost
hoar masking true punctuation of the fixed stars.

We held him in that dream, our loosed heat
thawing the geometry of his face,
his first-last words: *now I know of gravity*.

ELDER

I've been meaning to dig the elder out all day
but you see this small, fleshy fruiting
along the top of the south-facing branch?
That's Judas or wood ear, and it's edible –

soft and exact like your own pinna,
little helix curl, half-turned, as yours, asleep
amongst our gnarl of pillows and the numb crook
of my right arm. Darling, last night I lay

thinking through all the ways, and even if I give
everything with the billhook and axe then wreck
the ball of my foot on the lug-end of a spade
it'll take more than what's left of today.